Dear Sir,

MW00912381

Nuts And Bolts of Project Management

Thank you

804.833.7410

Nuts And Bolts of Project Management

Right Timing + Right Decision = SUCCESS

Srividhya Srinivasan IIM Bangalore
& Dr. Srivathsan Srinivasan

Library of Congress Control Number: 2009908439
ISBN: Hardcover   978-1-4415-6513-6
                       Softcover   978-1-4415-6512-9

This book was printed in the United States of America.

To order additional copies of this book, contact:
Xlibris Corporation
1-888-795-4274
www.Xlibris.com
Orders@Xlibris.com
67639

Table of Contents

With special thanks to friends and family for all their encouragement and support.

INTRODUCTION

T HIS BOOK, *NUTS and Bolts of Project Management,* is intended to provide basic know-how for novice and mid-level project managers in the IT industry. Beginning with the essentials of "What Is Project Management?" and "Who Is a Project Manager?" the book also details current thinking in project management processes and standards in terms of project scope definition, time and cost management, quality control, human resources, communication, risk and procurement management, and project integration. *Nuts and Bolts* also describes the complete project management life-cycle phases and shows how project management best practices can be applied in small and large firms.

The main purpose of the book is to help the reader understand project management practices by using simple illustrations for these sometimes difficult concepts. Emerging project managers may benefit most from learning these "nuts and bolts," but senior leaders may find the approach and examples used here to be useful in training their team members.

WHAT YOU'LL LEARN FROM THIS BOOK

THIS BOOK OFFERS complete knowledge of the basics of project management using easy-to-understand examples. The text provides good visibility into project management factors for emerging project managers, customers, and other project stakeholders. Topics covered include definition of project scope, time and cost management, quality control, human resources, communication, risk and procurement management, and project integration—explaining the complete project management life-cycle.

- Managing projects
- Initiating projects and planning toward successful closure
- Building a strong team
- Being a good team player
- Identifying resources and materials for a successful project
- Monitoring and controlling project budgets and timelines
- Managing changes that affect your project
- Closing out projects
- Learning from past project records

AUTHOR BIOGRAPHY

Srividhya Srinivasan, EGMP, IIM Bangalore

Industry Experience: Srividhya Srinivasan

- Diverse experience in all aspects of project management for both small organizations and companies. Has served as program manager to general managers and vice presidents, CMO.

Credentials:

- EGMB – IIM Bangalore
- Project Management Institute, Member
- Circle of Excellence Award
- Outstanding Performance Award
- Quality Point Certification on CMM – L5 Process

Speaking Engagements:

- Active participant in project management forums.
- Conducts project management seminars.
- Participates in interdepartmental presentations in various organizations.

Market Strategy:

Nuts and Bolts of Project Management fills a unique niche in the market of project management books. The work offers simple examples of real-world projects and includes reasons for success and failure, live application of project management factors, and best practices for experienced and emerging project managers in the IT industry.

This book may be used as a classroom reference guide for IT project management training because it presents various scenarios and easy-to-understand examples covering all aspects of project management: definition of project scope, time and cost management, quality control, human resources, communication, and risk and procurement management.

Srivathsan Srinivasan, BE, MS, PHD, USA

Industry Experience

- Dr. Srivathsan Srinivasan has varied experience in different technical domains in Fortune 500 companies. President and CEO of Prestigious Group Of Consultants LLC, A well established process management fi rm implementing 'BEST PRACTICES' of project management methodologies.

Credentials

- Dr. Srivathsan Srinivasan has implemented such projects as: IS0:9000 Quality Standards, Capability Maturity Model L 5i, Six Sigma, and Total Quality Management

Speaking Engagements

- Active participant in project management research forums.

Project Management: An Introduction

CHAPTER 1

A T 7:05 IN the evening, the phone rang and Sue's boyfriend, Mike, said, "Sue, would you like to go out to dinner with Chris and me?"

"Why not?" Sue thought.

An unplanned event. What's the first thing to do given that the time was already 7:05? INTIATE action, then plan for the evening:

> What to wear?
> How much money to carry?
> What will the weather be like later? Will it get cold enough to require a jacket?

Oops, another call: "We'll go downtown for dinner. Chris and I will meet at your house in exactly 30 minutes. Then, we'll all take my car to the restaurant."

Now, indeed, time was a major factor. Sue changed into her jeans and burgundy top, as planned, and dabbed on a bit of makeup.

The doorbell rang, and in a moment, Chris and Mike were standing in Sue's entry hall. "Hey, you look nice, Sue," said Mike. Within minutes, the three friends were driving toward the city.

Mike said, "Sue, have you thought about what type of food you'd like to have? There are tons of restaurants downtown: Chinese, Thai, Japanese . . ."

"Gosh," thought Sue, "everything from a basic morning walk to getting ready for bed at night needs planning. Life is like a complex project in itself." So she put a question to Mike: "Hey, Mike, you're a project manager. Tell me how you define a project and how you go about managing it. Is it all about initiation and planning alone?"

"Let's talk about that after we choose a restaurant," Mike replied.

After the group was comfortably seated in a good Italian restaurant and Sue had already started on a plate of fettuccini, Mike said, "Let's take a very simple example of project management, Sue. I just happened to call you at about 7:05 tonight. What did you do to get ready for dinner?"

"Well, time was short, and I had to think about what to wear, how much money to carry, whether it might get cold later and I would need to bring a jacket . . ."

"So you initiated a plan. Then what did you do?"

"I carried out my initially planned tasks, got ready on time, and here I am, out with you."

Mike said, "That's execution. Now, what did you do before leaving?"

Sue replied, "I ran through my final checklist: I made sure my hair was brushed, my makeup and clothes looked good, and I had my jacket, keys, and money."

Mike said, "That's the final closure of what you planned. Sue, a project can be anything, from building a toy train to launching a big rocket from NASA. With any project, you follow a set of processes to accomplish certain tasks. In a nutshell, project management is just managing processes with the help of tools in a well-organized way to accomplish certain goals."

Chris chimed in: "That's quite interesting, but don't you think you completely forgot about ways to control a project? In the IT industry, project controls are usually well defined and are considered part of the project management process."

Mike agreed: "Initiation and planning are just the beginning of the project management life-cycle process. Next comes execution of the tasks as per the original plan. In Sue's case, she might have had to cut down her time to accomplish certain tasks to be ready 30 minutes after I called. That's what we call project control."

Chris said, "You also forgot about risk mitigation and contingency planning."

Sue jumped in: "That's right. I took some money for dinner and a jacket in case it turned cold. Is that contingency planning?"

Mike said, "Sure, it is, Sue."

"Since Mike's the senior manager, sitting right next to us," said Chris, "let's let him decide what's for dessert." Sue and Mike laughed.

"Okay," said Mike, "Let's initiate and plan. First, what do we do?"

Sue answered: "Let's list what we all like to have, figure out whether it's the same, and place an order. Gee, that sounds like someone planning a party; is it really project initiation?"

"Yes, Sue," replied Mike. "You've just made a list of tasks to be carried out for this DESSERT project. Now you know what to accomplish for the DESSERT project, and finally, you have to develop your project charter."

"After that," said Chris, "we execute and place an order, right?"

Mike added: "Don't forget formal closure and, of course, last but not least, lessons learned."

Sue spoke up again: "We might need references, too. They always come in handy."

"That's it," said Mike. "That forms the nuts and bolts of the project management process." [See figure 1.1.]

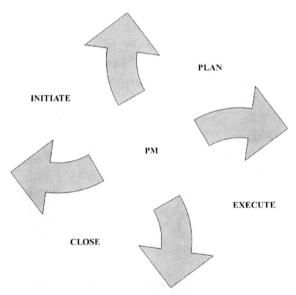

PLAN

INITIATE

PM

CLOSE

EXECUTE

Fig. 1.1 Project Management Processes

Back in the car, the three friends were happily stuffed and heading home.

Chris said, "Hey, Mike, back to the project management discussion: *Scope* is just addressing the requirements given by the customer, right?"

Sue asked, "Chris, what do you mean by 'just addressing'?"

Mike said, "Let's take an example here. When we placed an order for dessert, what did the waiter serve us?"

Sue answered, "Two orders of cream cheese cake and one chocolate crème."

"So we got exactly what we needed–nothing more and nothing less, right?"

"Yes."

Mike continued: "That's the basic meaning of *scope*: giving the customer exactly what he or she wants, nothing more, which could add time and costs to the project."

Chris said, "In my company, we organize the smaller sections or units of project work into a *work breakdown structure*."

"Yes, Chris. That's breaking down the project into smaller, more manageable activities or tasks. You start with the project name, then you need requirements analysis, design/development testing, and other tasks for a complete project life-cycle. The work breakdown structure, or WBS, forms the backbone of any project, small or large."

Sue said, "While we're talking about all this project management stuff, Mike, could you help me with time management? I don't think I'm very good at it."

Remembering his last project, Mike said, "Time management is a very difficult task. As a senior project manager, a big part of my job is scheduling project tasks. I have to look at activity sequencing, that is, lining up the activities in the order they should be performed, and I have to estimate the time frame for each activity."

The three friends had arrived back at Sue's house. She invited Mike and Chris in to continue the conversation.

Sue replied, "I heard a manager at work say that resource planning is the most crucial part of time management, but I've heard others talk about cost management. Are they both important?"

Chris chimed in: "A few years ago, my family and I were moving to a new house, so we called in packers and movers. Their manager assigned each worker to pack one room in the house. That was the work breakdown structure related to the scope of the project. In this case, *scope* meant packing the household things.

"The task breakdown was associated with various resource levels and the costs incurred by each of the resources for completing the tasks assigned to them. This analysis is usually done during the planning phase of a project.

"There are various methods involved in project estimation. For instance, you can use expert judgment, where you come to a conclusion based on past records. The moving company could estimate the time for workers to pack up and move a small, medium, or big household. With parametical estimation, mathematical models are used, and in bottom-up estimating, you look at the time taken to complete each individual task in a continuous way."

Mike was impressed with Chris's example. "Chris, in my experience as a project manager, we used to do budgeting for a project using the cost estimates based on the WBS and the time involved for the total completion of the project tasks by the project resources."

Sue grabbed a piece of paper and started sketching out a table. "In other words, we could use these estimates as inputs to budgeting–say, for a medium-sized house." [See table 1.1.]

Resource	Task: Pack household items	Estimate: Time required for task (hours)
R1	Front hall	4
R2	Dining room	3
R3	Bedroom	5
R4	Kitchen	3
R5	Game room	1
R6	Fitness room	2
R7	Computer room	1
R8	Guest room	2
R9	Children's room	4
R10	Storage room	5

Table 1.1 Schedule Estimation

Sue continued: "Then, we put together the work breakdown structure–that's cost associated with each activity. Right?"

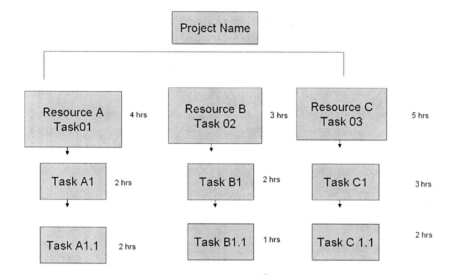

Figure 1.2–Work Breakdown Structure

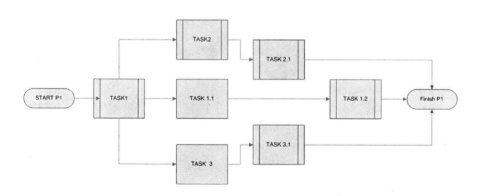

Figure 1.3–Activity Sequencing Diagram

Chris said, "That explains it all, Sue, excellent. Let's also think about how we keep the project on schedule."

Mike jumped in: "Here, we're talking about measuring performance and controlling project changes.

Sue asked, "Are we also talking about cost control processes?"

Mike said, "Exactly, Sue, you're absolutely right. At the same time, we have to think about quality assurance. For instance, what if it had rained hard tonight and the roads were slippery? I would have been glad that I spent the money for a good car with four-wheel drive so that we all got to the restaurant safely."

Chris said, "Quality management starts right from the planning phase of a project, mainly concentrating on the cost of quality, quality assurance, and quality control."

Sue looked confused. "Chris, you need to explain that to me in more detail."

Mike said, "Let me tell you about it, Sue. To make any good product that meets the quality requirements of its customer, we need to make sure we can meet the cost of the skilled resources and allow enough time. The money spent on making my car a quality product that could meet my requirements as a customer is the *cost of quality*."

Chris added, "And by *quality assurance*, we mean to say whether the product is made in accordance with the requirements of the customer in terms of quality, like whether the car gets good mileage, has special safety features, and so on, and whether it's made as per the quality processes established by the car manufacturing unit in considering customer needs."

Sue said, "I know the next one! *Quality control* is checking from time to time, from the start of building the car to completion, to see whether or not it meets the quality standards set by the car manufacturing firm in meeting the customer needs."

Mike laughed: "Good work! Sue, I could employ you on my next project." Then Mike continued: "What if a policeman had stopped us for speeding on the way to the restaurant?"

Sue replied, "Once I got stopped, but as I was talking to the policeman, we discovered that we were from the same hometown. He ended up being nice and not giving me a ticket–thank goodness!"

Chris said, "That just shows how important people management is in day-to-day life."

Mike remembered, "Many years ago, when I was first starting in my role as a project manager, a major obstacle for me was to manage my project team. The team members all came from different countries, spoke different languages, and were used to different behavior in the workplace. My senior manager, however, had high expectations for me. I learned to pay attention to human psychology. As one of my friends advised me: 'Try understanding others, then understand yourself.'"

Chris interrupted: "Developing a staffing management plan would have been your primary activity, right?"

Very true, Chris, and that's not as easy as it might seem to be. The first thing to do is to document all the interfaces in the project, then look into the staffing needs, basically to see what kinds of resources are needed for the project and what types of tasks should be assigned to them. There might also be limitations in using project resources as the project manager wants to, such as organizational influences or setup."

Sue asked, "Are you talking about resources as major constraints in the staffing plan?"

Mike replied, "Exactly Sue; you're right. Acquiring the right kind of staff is the key for human resource management. Negotiating and building the project team is a major task in any project."

Chris added, "Assigning appropriate roles and responsibilities is another major factor to be considered. In my previous project, we couldn't meet the deadlines because we were unable to find suitable resources for the requirements. Finally, we came up with these inputs for the staffing management plan." Chris sketched out a quick figure on Sue's scrap paper (figure 1.4).

Business Unit	R1/T1	R2/T2	R3/T3
BFSI	2	4	8
Insurance	2	4	8
Transportation	1	2	4

Figure 1.4–Staffing Management Plan(Inputs)
Note: R1 stands Resource 1 and T1 stands for Task 1

"Team building is an art in itself," declared Mike. "But for teamwork, we wouldn't have made it to the restaurant on time. What do you say, Sue?" Figure 1.4a TEAM BUILDING PYRAMID.

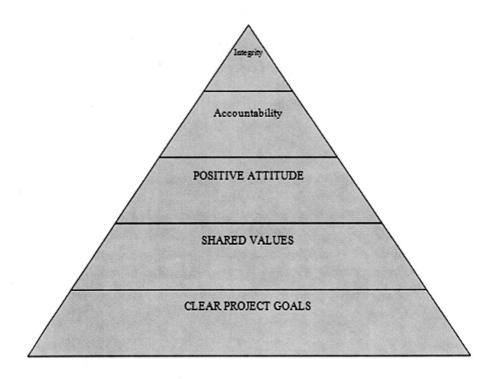

Figure 4.1a–TEAM BUILDING PYRAMID

"I agree, Mike. Any project, from planning a meal at your kitchen table to building an aircraft, needs strong teamwork. Does team building begin as soon as a new project team is formed?"

Chris said, "That's right, Sue. In my company, one way we tackle conflicts in project teams is to have frequent team-building activities, like training or just getting together for a party. That way, all team members are able to meet and get to know each other well."

Mike chimed in: "Speaking of parties, how about let's turn on the TV and have something to drink, Sue?"

Sue flipped on the TV, then went to the kitchen to fix drinks. When she returned, Mike and Chris were talking about the role of good communication in project management.

Sue said, "I didn't realize communication was so important in working on a project; I thought the main goal was to get your own tasks completed."

Mike interrupted: "Sue, I asked for cocktail, but you've given me a mocktail."

Chris burst out in a loud laughter: "Now do you understand, Sue? It's essential to convey the right message to the right person at the right time."

"You should also know which type of communication to use, such as direct or indirect; whether to communicate formally or informally; and so on. Here's a chart we use in my office," said Mike, as he added to the sketches on Sue's coffee table (see figure 1.5).

COMMUNICATION CHANNELS	DIRECT	INDIRECT	FORMAL	INFORMAL	INTERNAL / EXTERNAL
WHAT					
WHOM					
WHEN					
WHERE					
HOW					

Figure 1.5–Methods of 'COMMUNICATION'

At last, Chris rose to leave. Sue said, "Hey, Chris, it looks like it's getting colder out there. I hope you were as smart as I was and brought a jacket with you."

Chris replied, "I've got a jacket in the car. After all we've learned about project management tonight, I can add that anticipating that it might be cold is risk mitigation, and bringing a jacket is contingency planning."

Sue said, "I think that's enough project management for tonight, Chris, thanks."

After Chris left, Sue turned to Mike and teased, "What kind of risk mitigation do we need to do before we get married?"

Mike replied, "Well, if you really want to know, there are a few aspects that we need to keep in mind for any risk statement: risk identification, risk prioritization, and risk response planning. Those form the basis for developing your risk management plan." (See table 1.3.)

1	Risk identification
2	Risk prioritization
3	Risk response planning

Table 1.3 Inputs for Risk Management Plan

Sue asked, "What's risk response planning?"

"It's the most important element of the risk management process. First, you need to know the risks and analysis of the risks involved and various risk responses from the project team. You might have to change the project schedule, cost, or time–the triple constraints–revolving the time over the project as per the risk responses. Then, you review the risk responses and come up with contingency plans. Here's another little sketch we use in my office to clarify." (See figure 1.6.)

Project Name   **Date**

RISK DESCRIPTION	RISK LEVEL	RISK RESPONSE	OWNER

Figure 1.6–RISK RESPONSE PLAN

Sue said, "That's great, risk management in a nutshell."

"Hey, did I mention you look great tonight, Sue?"

"Thanks, honey. I bought this top at Carolyn's store. Do you remember her? She's a retailer."

"Now, you're talking about procurement management."

"Oh, no, more project management? Just explain, please."

"Here's another example, Sue: What do we need to do to plan for our wedding?"

"Well, there are lots of arrangements to make. I mean, looking for a dress, booking a hotel for the reception, ordering invitations . . ."

"What if I said I have a better idea? We can contract all that work out to a wedding planning agency. How does that sound to you?"

"That'd be great!"

"First, we need to decide the type of contract we want for our WEDDING project, and we have to make sure we have a good plan to procure and manage the project financially and technically."

"Hey, are you asking me . . . ?"

"Back to the real world. At my office, we have various types of contracts: *Fixed price* means that the client pays a fixed price for the work provided by the contractor. In a *cost-reimbursable contract*, the client reimburses the contractor for all the costs."

"That sounds like quite a risky venture, Mike."

"Yes, it is, because you don't know how much the total cost for your project will be. That's definitely more beneficial to the contractor than it is to you. The last type of contract is *time and materials*, which is a blend of fixed-price and cost-reimbursable contract types. Procurement planning is a discipline in itself. You need to know how to evaluate proposals, how to select vendors, and how to manage vendors and contracts."

"At work, the managers are always talking about the statement of work. How important is that in procurement management?"

"The statement of work, or SOW, is needed for every service or product a company procures. It helps your company get the best deal for products or services. It's always better if the SOW is clear and precise for all project stakeholders to avoid any confusion later."

"What do the senior managers mean by 'project integration'?"

"That's a crucial factor for developing a project plan. It means that you have all the aspects of your project in place: scope, time, cost, quality, risk, change management process, release management process, organizational policies, and so on."

"So once you have a baseline plan, you take the Professional responsibility of executing it as per the project plan, right?"

"You got it, Sue!"

"Okay, I think now I know the nuts and bolts—the fundamentals—of project management."

Initiation Phase

CHAPTER 2

AFTER MIKE FINALLY got off the topic of project management and asked Sue to marry him, the wedding was beautiful. Now, the time had come for the couple to buy their first house.

Mike said, "Let's talk to Tim about our house-hunting project. You'll be the project manager, Sue, so what do you think your first step should be?"

"To initiate a process?"

"What do you mean?"

"To verify whether or not we have the required information for our project, that is, project requirements, then to understand the scope of the project and to come up with a scope statement and identify the documents or deliverables that will be needed. We also have to form a project team and come up with a project charter. Is that right, honey?"

Mike was busily drawing another figure on a piece of paper. "That's right, Sue. And you can always refer to this drawing if you still have doubts."

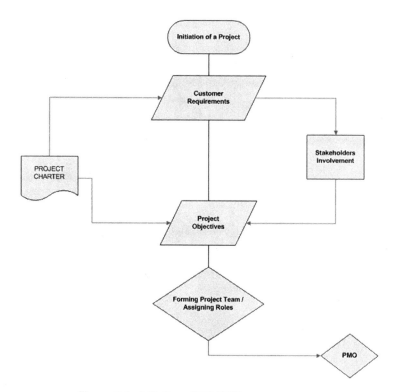

Figure : 2.1 – Initiating a 'PROJECT'

Mike continued: "Let's jump-start our HOUSE-HUNTING project. Our goal is to buy a nice house. First, let's make a list of things we need to know."

> ➤ Who are the key stakeholders of the project?
> ➤ What are the project requirements?
> ➤ What kind of resources do we need for our project?
> ➤ What will be the roles and responsibilities of our resource team members?
> ➤ Where will the project funding come from?
> ➤ What will be the final outcome of the project?

Project Stakeholders:

By *stakeholders*, we mean all the team members, the customer or sponsor of the project, project designers, developers, testers, and so on. In this case, Mike and Sue are the key stakeholders. Other stakeholders include the real-estate agent, homeowners (sellers), home inspectors, and attorneys.

Project Sponsor:

The project sponsor provides the complete funding for the project. He or she approves the feasibility plan for the project and releases funds to complete the project successfully. Before the allocation of senior project managers to a project, the project sponsor must be in place. Responsibilities of the project sponsor include the following:

> ➤ Ensures that all project stakeholders understand the scope of the project.
> ➤ Communicates and develops a business case in favor of completing the project.
> ➤ Analyzes and approves the project estimates given by senior managers.
> ➤ Works with the project manager to develop the project charter.
> ➤ Approves the project charter.

PROJECT CHARTER
PROJECT NAME
PROJECT OBJECTIVES
BUSINESS CASE
STAKEHOLDERS ROLE
PROJECT BUDGET
PROJECT SPONSOR Approval   PROJECT MANAGER Approval

Figure 2.2–PROJECT CHARTER

For Mike and Sue's HOUSE-HUNTING project, the bank plays the role of the project sponsor.

Project Requirements:

For Mike and Sue, the project requirements are as follows:

- ➤ To determine the budget and time for purchase of a new home.
- ➤ To determine the model of the house.
- ➤ To decide on the location for the house.
- ➤ To ensure the quality of materials used in the house.
- ➤ To secure funding.

Requirements analysis will be done by Sue and Mike, who are the key stakeholders in the project.

Other Stakeholders:

The real-estate agent's responsibilities are as follows:

- ➤ To find out if chosen house models are available in the location and at the price Mike and Sue desire.
- ➤ To show various houses in that category for approval.
- ➤ To get final approval.

As mentioned earlier, the bank plays a crucial role in funding for this project. Its responsibilities include the following:

- ➤ To investigate whether Sue and Mike are eligible for the applied loan amount to fund the house.
- ➤ To ensure that Mike and Sue are able to repay the loan within the said period to the bank.

An attorney will also play an active role in the project. Responsibilities of the attorney include the following:

- ➤ To ensure that the loan documents are completed per the bank policies and meet all the requisite criteria for funding.
- ➤ To ensure that the purchase of the house complies with rules and regulations of the government.
- ➤ To help draft an agreement document between buyer and seller.

The home inspector has these responsibilities:

➢ To determine whether or not the electric lines are working properly and to ensure that the house has no plumbing or other structural problems.
➢ To ensure that the building materials and home structure meet the requirements of Mike and Sue.

Figure 2.3 shows the resources needed and roles played in this project.

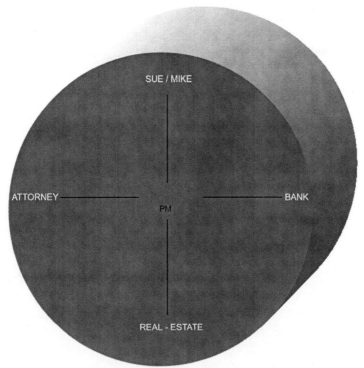

Figure : 2.3 – Project Stakeholders (House Hunting Project)

Note : Project Manager's role would be revolving around project stakeholders to control the project as per the Project Management Plan

Outcome of the Project:

Sue and Mike hope to find a beautiful, four-bedroom home in Centreville, Virginia, close to shopping, schools, and hospitals. If they achieve that goal, all the project requirements will have been met successfully.

Role of the Project Manager:

> ➤ Understand the requirements of the project and work with the project sponsor to define the scope, schedule, and budget.
> ➤ Resource and manage project deliveries.
> ➤ Maintain the effectiveness of the working team.
> ➤ Monitor and control project activities.
> ➤ Participate in the final sign-off approvals for formal closure of the project.
> ➤ Maintain historical records for future reference.

Project Planning

CHAPTER 3

SUE AND MIKE were relaxing after a long day on the house hunt when the doorbell rang. Sue opened the door to see her father-in-law, Steve, on the doorstep. He was a tall, slim man, always ready to help out and give advice to his children.

Steve said, "I heard you two are looking to buy a new home. I thought I'd drop by to give you some guidance."

"Come on in," Sue replied. "We need all the help we can get."

Mike said, "Dad, we've already arranged for financing and employed a real-estate agent who is working on our requirements."

"Son, do you have a plan in place for your market approach? What kind of budgeting have you done? Have you spoken to some of your friends who have recently bought homes in Centreville? Are their homes similar to the one you have in mind? How many houses have you seen so far? Who's your agent, and what kind of experience does he have in this industry?"

"Dad, you should be proud of us. We already have our analysis report in place."

"Son, I'm glad to see you're putting into practice all I taught you about project management before you even stepped into the business world. You're nowhere without planning, planning, and planning. Do you remember the steps involved in planning?"

"Sure, Dad. Before developing the project management plan, you need to know:

> ➢ The scope of the project
> ➢ The time needed to complete the project
> ➢ The costs involved to complete the project
> ➢ The quality requirements as they relate to the business, customer, or organizational need
> ➢ The number and types of resources required by the project
> ➢ The type of communication needed among project stakeholders to make the project a success
> ➢ The types of risks involved and contingency plans for addressing the risks
> ➢ The roles and responsibilities of the resources at the initial stages of the project.

"And, Dad, I remember you said that the project plan is an integration of all these factors under one manager."

Steve said, "I'm proud of you, Son. But what happens if changes come up in the project? Suppose, for example, you decide to buy a larger house?"

"Well, Dad, in my experience as a senior manager at work, we have a change control board, or CCB, to handle upcoming changes in our projects."

Sue chimed in: "Can you please explain that? I don't think I understand."

Mike answered, "Sue, in any project, a group of stakeholders forms what's called a change control board. The CCB tells you whether or not the proposed changes to the project should be considered. Here's another one of my sketches to show you how the CCB works." (See figure 3.1.)

SNO	DATE	VERSION NUMBER	CHANGE	AUTHOR

Figure 3.1–Change Control Index

Teasing Mike, Sue asked, "Honey, am I one of the members of the CCB?"

"Of course, you are sweetie . . . the main one."

The room filled with loud laughter.

Later, as Sue fixed dinner, Mike showed Steve the analysis report he and Sue had written for house-hunting.

Steve commented, "Looks good to me. You can also keep it as a baseline project plan for the HOUSE HUNTING project. An approved project charter acts as the basic tool for planning. Once you have that in place and are clear about your goals, you start building your project team. Then, it's onto the . . ."

"Work breakdown structure," interjected Sue.

"That's right, Sue. Where'd you learn that?"

Smiling at Mike, Sue said, "I have to give credit to our handy project manager at home . . . 24/7/365 . . ." Then she continued, "But, Mike, I don't think you've taught me about tools for project planning."

"There are tons of tools and techniques, Sue, but probably two of the most important are the Gantt chart and PERT analysis. Gantt charts are just like bar diagrams that tell you when tasks will begin and end and give complete descriptions of the tasks. In other words, the Gantt chart tells you how to time your tasks to complete the project work. [See figures3.2 and 3.3.]

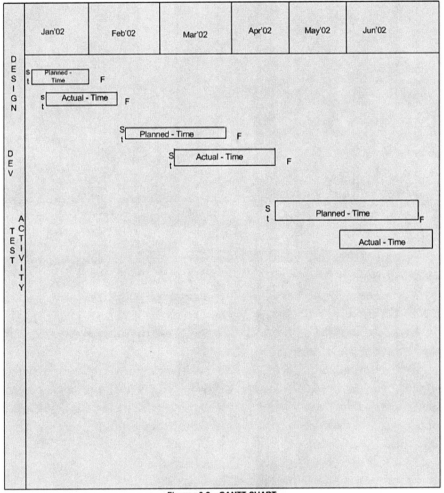

Figure : 3.2 – GANTT CHART

Note : St stands for 'START DATE' and F stands for 'FINISH DATE' of an activity.

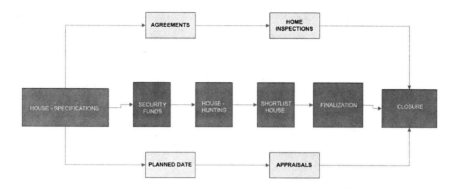

Figure : 3.3 – PERT (House hunting Project)

Note : ▮ depicts the 'CRITICAL PATH' and ▯ depicts 'NON-CRITICAL PATH' analysis of the 'House- hunting' project.

"In a Gantt chart, each task is represented by a row, and the rows are incremented by days, weeks, or months, according to the project activities. Horizontal bars show the progress of the activities with the beginning dates and completion dates. *Milestones* are the events of significance occurring in the project."

Steve said, "Mike, let me tell her about PERT analysis. Back in the 1950s, to handle the complexity of larger projects, we old-timers developed a network model for project management for the U.S. Navy Polaris project, which had thousands of contractors. The basic aim of this *Program Evaluation and Review Technique*, or PERT, analysis was to reduce the time and costs of projects. [See figure 3.3.]

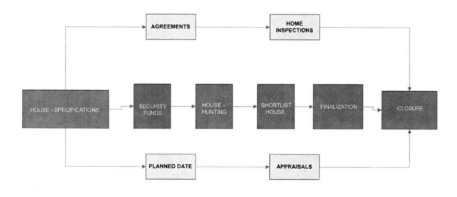

Figure : 3.3 – PERT (House hunting Project)

Note : ▮ depicts the 'CRITICAL PATH' and ▯ depicts 'NON-CRITICAL PATH' analysis of the 'House- hunting' project.

"PERT is an activity-based diagram in which you represent the activity on lines and milestones on nodes. It's also known as an *activity-on-node diagram*."

Sue said, "I'm not sure I understand."

Mike answered, "It's very simple, Sue. Let's do a PERT planning session.

> ➢ First of all, you have to identify the activities or tasks and milestones for completion of your project.
> ➢ Next, you arrange the activities sequentially and estimate the time for each activity.
> ➢ You then develop a network of activities.
> ➢ Finally, you calculate the critical path."

Sue asked, "What's critical path analysis, Mike?"

"When you conduct CPA, you calculate the time allocated for completing each task of the project, or you can think of it is the total calendar time required for project completion. The time span in which the non-critical path can get delayed without affecting or delaying the project is called *slack time*. We use a chart like this at work to estimate time for project activities."

Table 3.1

Early Start Time	The earliest time an activity or task can START, keeping in view activities that precede this task.
Early Finish Time	The earliest time an activity or task can FINISH, keeping in view activities that precede this task.
Late Start Time	The time in which an activity can START without affecting the project schedule.
Late Finish Time	The time in which an activity can FINISH without affecting the project schedule.

Steve patted his son on the shoulder. "Good work, Mike. I think you understand the nuts and bolts of project management for buying your first house."

Project Execution (Monitoring and Control)

CHAPTER 4

LATER THAT NIGHT, after Steve left, Sue said, "Mike, I still have so many unanswered questions in my mind about finding a new house."

"What do you mean, Sue?"

"For instance, how are we going to monitor and control this project?"

Even though Mike was tired, he knew that good managers are on call 24*7*365. He answered Sue: "To initiate any kind of project management control process, you should have a baseline project plan with all the project information on scope, cost, time, quality, risks, and so on."

"What are the main things we need to look into, Mike?"

"First, we need to form a good working project team whose members are committed and experienced in PMC processes. The rest of it . . . we'll have to deal with in the morning."

. . .

The next morning, Sunday, Steve came by for another visit, along with Mike's mother, Martha. At just about the same time, Chris showed up on Mike and Sue's doorstep.

Chris asked, "What's the progress on your house-hunting project, Sue?"

Sue said, "You're just in time, Chris. Mike and Steve are having a serious discussion on monitoring and controlling the project. Mike only told me about the first few steps in the process. Maybe you could fill me in on the rest."

Chris replied, "Sure, Sue. Once the project information is baselined in the project management plan, we have adequate project information from our SMP (Scope Management Plan), CMP (Cost Management Plan), TMP (Time Management Plan), communication management plan, QMP (Quality Management Plan), RMP (Risk Management Plan) inputs in the project management plan as per the objectives of the project in place.

We also have to ensure that all the contract agreement documents are in place."

Mike added, "The project is monitored as per the project management plan. You also have to remember that all project stakeholders are equally important in the PMC process for successful completion of the project.

Chris said, "It's the project manager's sole responsibility to use the project information and resources to control the project. The project manager has to keep a constant check on the project status, including all the activities in the project executed by the resources, by using various PMC tools and techniques, such as performance measurement indexes and daily, weekly, or monthly project status reports."

Steve said, "As a project manager, you also have to coordinate with the CCB and bring the changes in the project under control. Your duties are not just not limited to scope, cost, schedule, risk mitigation, milestones, or project agreement documents, but you have to use your communication skills to fill in the gaps among all the project stakeholders. This can be a major undertaking in many projects."

"In monitoring a project," added Mike, "you must also know how the project is deviating from the actual plan. A good example would be comparing what was originally planned to the present status by using review methodologies. I call this looking at actual vs. planned."

- Actual vs. Planned (cost variances)
- Actual vs. Planned (schedule variances)
- Actual vs. Planned (risks encountered, contingencies in place)
- Actual vs. Planned (% involvement of stakeholders until the end of the project)

"As a project manager," said Chris, "you must verify whether or not the changes occurring in the project are to be considered and make a joint decision with the CCB and the project team." [See figure 4.1.]

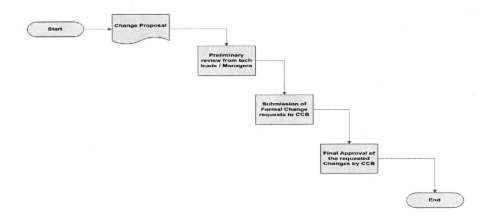

Figure 4.1–Change Control Process
Note: CCB stands for 'Change Control Board'

Sue put in: "Finally, you document the needed corrections in the project, right, guys?"

Together, Steve, Mike, and Chris said, "Right, Sue!"

Mike continued, "Then, the last step would be to document the changes occurring and the corrections made to successfully complete the project work."

Sue asked, "Honey, can you give me some examples of PMC processes?"

"First, Sue, ask yourself these questions:

➤ How do you measure the performance of your project?
➤ What was planned and what is the actual progress of project work?
➤ How do you verify project deliverables from time to time during the project?
➤ How do you perform effort estimations of resources per the given tasks?
➤ What amount of re-work do you need to do to complete your project?

"Your answers to those questions will show you the processes you need to undertake."

[See figure 4.2.]

SNO	RNAME	ACTIVITY	PDOC	ADOC	COMMENTS

Figure 4.2–PROJECT ACTIVITY CHART

Note: RNAME stands for 'Name of the Resource'
PDOC–'Planned date of Completion'
ADOC–'Actual date of Completion'

"Wait a minute," said Steve, "what acts as inputs to the PMC documents?"

Mike answered, "Good question Dad. The answer is not as simple as it might seem. Let's see, you need:

➤ Cost estimates, schedule variances, activities or tasks, critical path information, and milestones
➤ Actual project information or data
➤ Technical input from project deliverables.

"The output would be your approved or completed plans on updated project information."

"To sum up," said Chris, "As a project manager, you should, first, conduct regular team meetings with all project stakeholders—customers, senior managers, sponsors, technical team members, and business heads. You should also motivate the project team by having fun get-togethers and creating opportunities for introverts to open up and extroverts to expand their ideas. You have to have reward programs in place for employees and keep an eye on the status of the project to make it a success.

"Second, as a project manager, you must always be aware of all the tasks, large and small, to be performed by the project resources. Any problems should be addressed immediately to save time and costs.

"Third, as you both stated earlier, the project manager has to look into the action items and change requests, take corrective actions, and document them for future reference.

"Fourth, you have to make sure that all the project stakeholders are aware of the current status of the project.

"Fifth, it's your responsibility to see that the current project work meets all the customer requirements as per the signed agreements, such as delivery dates, processes, and standards.

"Sixth, you have to resolve any issues with the customer in accepting deliverables.

"Finally, you record past corrective actions that may be used in the future."

"That about sums it up, Chris," said Steve. "You're almost as knowledgeable about project management as my son, Mike."

Closing out Project Work

CHAPTER 5

B EFORE MIKE AND Sue left for another round of house-hunting, Sue said, "The thing I'm looking forward to most is closure of our new house project. I think even I can explain this phase of project management.

"Let's use the example of a friendly tea-making project. Once we have the utensils and ingredients ready for preparing the tea, we get into execution: We boil water, add tea bags, and prepare to serve the tea with sugar cubes.

"Before we bring the tea to our guests, we make sure that we've completed all the tasks required for making the tea. Similarly, when a project manager closes out a project, he or she needs to make sure that all tasks have been completed per the plan."

"That's rightly stated, Sue," said Mike. "In real-world scenarios, once you have sign-off approvals for all project deliverables from the customer and project team, you keep the deliverables as historical records, or *lessons learned*, for the next upcoming project. Then, you release the resources on the project."

Chris added, "In my company, we follow a set of prescribed steps:

> ➤ The project manager has to conduct an audit as the first step in formal closure.
> ➤ If the project is not complete or a phase has been eliminated, the project manager must provide justification.

> ➤ The manager has to receive formal approval from the customer or sponsor for project closure.
> ➤ Finally, the project manager must document lessons learned.

"Once the project has been completed per the statements in the contract agreement, the project manager makes sure that the organization gets the final payoff from the customer before project closure."

The group was so involved in the project management discussion that hardly anyone noticed Mike's mother, Martha, speaking on the telephone.

"I've got great news," Martha announced. "You've finally got project closure, Sue. That was our realtor on the phone. Steve and I are giving you the home you wanted as a gift."

The room erupted in expressions of surprise and happiness. Sue didn't know who to hug first: her husband, her in-laws, or even Chris!

Knowledge Management

CHAPTER 6

A FEW YEARS later, Sue and Mike were recovering from a birthday party for their five-year-old daughter, Sarah. Within minutes, the house had been flooded with kids moving at top speed and energy.

Sarah was happy to see her friends, and Mike had recorded the event with his video camera. There had been a bridal-doll ice-cream cake placed in the middle of the table, surrounded by goodie bags for the guests. Sarah, dressed as Snow White, blew out the candles and helped serve the cake as her little princess friends applauded.

Later, after the guests left and Sarah was asleep, Sue said to Mike, "We should put together an album for Sarah with her first schoolwork, the pictures she draws, the cards she gets for her birthday . . ."

Mike agreed: "You're right, Sue. We call that data storage at work."

Sue teased: "Mike, are you going to go off about project management again?"

"Knowledge is any day power, sweetie, and learning is a continuous process. People should be learning all the time. To learn, you need data or information on the activity you're interested in, and to share your learning and benefit others, you need to store the information in a central area or repository that is accessible to all."

Sue said, "Okay, I'll play along with you. If it hadn't been for Michelle, Sarah's birthday would not have been so nice."

"Why do you say that?"

"Michelle helped me plan for our little one's party. She had quite a lot of information on where to buy the cake for an affordable price, where to get Sarah's Snow White dress, and where to find party plates, balloons, and so on."

"See? That's what we call meaningful information, or knowledge, for kids' parties. Similarly, at work, we store our project-related information or data in a central knowledge area or link that is accessible to all employees in various departments."

"One important aspect of knowledge management is learning from past data. Do you agree, Mike?"

"Absolutely! Once, during project budgeting, I got caught up in the middle of a banking project. I had to work on the previous quarter's profit-and-loss statement, but I didn't know the formulas well. The help manual and previous analysis processes stored in the central repository really pulled me through!"

"Thank goodness you survived," laughed Sue. "Now, can we go to bed, Mr. Project Manager? It's been a long day."

With that, peace and harmony fell over Sue and Mike's home.

Question and Answer

1. What is a project?

    A. A project is a task with a definite beginning and definite ending.
    B. A project is the ongoing process of project management.
    C. Both A and B
    D. None of the above

    Answer: A

2. How do you define the term "operations"?

    A. It refers to the various functional areas of a corporation.
    B. It is a process that takes place as necessary.
    C. It is a continuous process.
    D. None of the above

    Answer: C

3. How would you define the project management process?

    A. The project management process is the application of various tools and techniques to accomplish the requirements of project work.
    B. The process involves how you manage yourself in a project.
    C. The process involves how you manage a task.
    D. None of the above

    Answer: A

4. Name the different phases in the project management process.

    A. Initiation, planning, execution (monitoring and control), closure
    B. Initiation, planning, closure
    C. Initiation, execution, closure
    D. None of the above

    Answer: A

5. How much time is needed for completion of any given project work?

   A. The time required depends on the project manager's point of view.
   B. The time required depends on the size of the project or the number of tasks, as per the project requirements.
   C. The time required depends on the project team's point of view.
   D. None of the above

   Answer: B

6. Why do some projects require more time for completion?

   A. Unexpected resource crunch
   B. Unexpected changes from the customer
   C. Both A and B
   D. None of the above

   Answer: C

7. It is important for the project manager to make his expectations clear:

   A. To the project team in meeting the project deadlines
   B. To the sponsor
   C. To the people outside the project
   D. None of the above

   Answer: A

8. The project management plan is used to:

   A. Organize all the project activities as per the triple constraint and in accordance with quality control requirements
   B. Evaluate the performance of the team members
   C. Conduct project status meetings
   D. None of the above

   Answer: A

9. The project manager is formally assigned in the:

   A. Project plan document
   B. Risk mitigation document
   C. Project charter document
   D. None of the above

   Answer: C

10. The SOW is developed from:

    A. The scope statement
    B. The WBS
    C. Both A and B
    D. None of the above

    Answer: C

11. The project management plan includes the:

    A. Project management strategy
    B. WBS
    C. Cost and schedule estimates
    D. All of the above

    Answer: D

12. The following are project stakeholders except:

    A. Project manager
    B. Customer
    C. Project team
    D. Corporate HR staff

    Answer: D

13. Project stakeholders:

   A. Most of the time have a positive impact on the project work
   B. Can have a positive or negative impact on the project
   C. Generally have little impact on the outcome of the project
   D. None of the above

   Answer: A

14. A project manager should have:

   A. A complete understanding of all the project processes and methodologies
   B. A complete understanding of his or her responsibilities as a project manager
   C. The ability to deliver
   D. All of the above

   Answer: D

15. Which of the following statements is correct in terms of a project?

   A. Project management is an ongoing process.
   B. Project management is basically just knowing the risks involved in a project.
   C. Project management is all about knowing the quality standards in a project.
   D. A project has a definite beginning and end.

   Answer: D

16. A review at the end of a project phase is called:

   A. Phase exit
   B. Quitting phase
   C. Phase end
   D. All of the above

   Answer: A

17. The decisions of which entity listed below are crucial in a project?

    A. A team member
    B. People outside the project
    C. The project manager
    D. None of the above

    Answer: C

18. The application of various tools and techniques to accomplish a goal is called:

    A. The project management process
    B. The scope management process
    C. The risk management process
    D. None of the above

    Answer: A

19. Which one of the following is not a best practice in project management?

    A. Being proactive
    B. Motivating and inspiring
    C. Leading
    D. Keeping goals or strategies loose and undefined

    Answer: D

20. Which of the following are constraints in project management?

    A. Cost estimations
    B. Timeline definitions
    C. Both A and B
    D. None of the above

    Answer: C

21. A tangible product or service that partially or completely fulfills project requirements is called a:

    A. Project deliverable
    B. Project team
    C. Project manager
    D. None of the above

    Answer: A

22. Which of the following are the most important contributors to a successful project?

    A. Active and meaningful coordination among the members of the project team
    B. Communication gaps among the members of the project team
    C. A well-motivated team
    D. Both A and C

    Answer: D

23. Which of the following statements is true?

    A. Project management involves guiding the project successfully through all project phases.
    B. Project management involves keeping the project team happy.
    C. Project management involves keeping senior management happy.
    D. None of the above

    Answer: A

24. 'Operation' is:

    A. Part of the project management process
    B. Part of the risk management process
    C. is a continuous process
    D. None of the above

    Answer: C

25. How do you know if the project goals have been accomplished?

    A. The project requirements have been met and the project has come
       to a successful completion.
    B. The initial project tasks have been completed.
    C. The customer is happy with the progress of the project.
    D. None of the above

    Answer: A

26. Who is the project manager?

    A. A representative from upper-level management
    B. The person responsible for accomplishing the project goals
    C. The customer
    D. None of the above

    Answer: B

27. Who is responsible for project deliveries?

    A. Project team members
    B. The project manager along with the project team
    C. The customer
    D. None of the above

    Answer: B

28. The project manager directs the project work:

    A. as per the established requirements
    B. as per his or her own objectives and agenda
    C. as per the project team's advice
    D. None of the above

    Answer: A

29. A project manager's responsibilities do not include:

    A. Identifying project requirements
    B. Establishing achievable objectives
    C. Anticipating risks and developing contingencies
    D. Performing tasks that do not relate to the project

    Answer: D

30. What are the triple constraints in a project?

    A. Scope, time, cost
    B. Scope, time, risk
    C. Scope, time, quality
    D. None of the above

    Answer: A

31. One of the project manager's main responsibilities is to ensure effective communication:

    A. Among the various project groups
    B. With the customer only
    C. With upper-level management only
    D. All of the above

    Answer: A

32. The project management life cycle is defined as:

    A. The various phases of project work that must be completed to attain a certain goal
    B. The initiation and closure phases of the project work
    C. The execution phase of the project
    D. None of the above

    Answer: A

33. How do you define the term "integration management" in a project?

   A. The process of coordinating the different components of project management
   B. The process of motivating the project team members
   C. The process of identifying project risks
   D. All of the above

   Answer: A

34. Who is solely responsible for bringing the project to success?

   A. Customer
   B. Project team
   C. Project manager
   D. None of the above

   Answer: C

35. A project manager must be:

   A. An efficient negotiator
   B. An efficient performer in meeting project deliveries
   C. A reactive beast
   D. None of the above

   Answer: B

36. A project manager should be able to:

   A. Say no gracefully when necessary
   B. Say yes to all requests
   C. Say no on a whim because he or she is the one in charge
   D. None of the above

   Answer: A

37. The project management plan is created by the project manager with the help of:

    A. The project team
    B. The sponsor
    C. Both A and B
    D. None of the above

    Answer: A

38. To manage a group of related projects in a coordinated way is:

    A. Project management
    B. Program management
    C. Both A and B
    D. None of the above

    Answer: B

39. Which of the following is a centralized unit that organizes and plans the execution of projects effectively in an organization?

    A. PMC
    B. PMO
    C. CCB
    D. None of the above

    Answer: B

40. What organizational unit identifies the best practices and standards of project management in an organization?

    A. CMO
    B. TMO
    C. PMO
    D. None of the above

    Answer: C

41. Stakeholders are of high importance in a project because:

    A. They are involved in all the important project decisions.
    B. They include the sponsor, the project manager, the team members, and the customer.
    C. They can all do whatever they want, whenever they want.
    D. None of the above

    Answer: A

42. A project manager must have a good understanding of:

    A. The initiation phase of the project work
    B. The planning phase of the project work
    C. The execution and closure phases of the project work
    D. All of the above

    Answer: D

43. State the order of occurrence of the phases in project management.

    A. Initiation, planning, execution (monitoring and controlling), closure
    B. Planning, initiation, execution, closure
    C. Execution, initiation, planning, closure
    D. None of the above

    Answer: A

44. The WBS is:

    A. An important tool in the project management process
    B. Not mandatory
    C. Used if the project manager decides to do so
    D. None of the above

    Answer: A

45. Project status meetings are conducted by:

    A. The project manager
    B. The project team
    C. The customer
    D. None of the above

Answer: A

INITIATION

1. Describe the initiation phase of the project management process.

   A. Initiation is the end phase for each project.
   B. Initiation is the beginning of the project management phase, during which the project charter and scope statement are developed.
   C. The scope management plan is developed in this phase.
   D. None of the above

   Answer: B

2. Defining project roles and responsibilities is a part of:

   A. Initiation
   B. Planning
   C. Execution
   D. Closure

   Answer: A

3. Who is responsible for funding in a project?

   A. Project team
   B. Project Sponsor
   C. Project manager
   D. None of the above

   Answer: B

4. It's a good practice to do risk analysis:

   A. Toward the beginning of the project work
   B. In the middle of the project work
   C. At the end of the project work
   D. None of the above

   Answer: A

5. A project objective should be included in the:

   A. Risk plan
   B. Quality plan
   C. Project charter
   D. None of the above

   Answer: C

6. The project charter acts as input for:

   A. Scope definition
   B. Risk definition
   C. Quality definition
   D. None of the above

   Answer: A

7. The project charter authorizes a:

   A. Task
   B. Project manager to lead a project
   C. Resource
   D. None of the above

   Answer: B

8. Adopting "expert judgment":

   A. Is a best practice for all project managers.
   B. Is not a good practice of project management.
   C. Is unnecessary; project managers can rely on their own views
      instead.
   D. None of the above

   Answer: A

9. Initiation is the:

    A. Execution of any project
    B. Ending phase of any project
    C. Beginning phase of any project
    D. None of the above

    Answer: C

10. The following deliverable formally authorizes a project manager to lead a project:

    A. Quality management plan
    B. Project management plan
    C. Scope management plan
    D. Project charter

    Answer: D

11. Which of the following is not a part of the initiation phase in a project?

    A. Development of the project management plan
    B. Development of the scope statement
    C. Development of the project charter
    D. All of the above

    Answer: A

12. Stakeholder analysis is done in the:

    A. Initiation phase
    B. Planning phase
    C. Execution phase
    D. Closure phase

    Answer: A

13. You are in the process of gathering information to start building a toy train for a toy manufacturing company. Which phase of project management are you in?

    A. Initiation
    B. Planning
    C. Execution
    D. Closure

    Answer: A

14. A feasibility study is a part of:

    A. Initiation
    B. Planning
    C. Execution
    D. Closure

    Answer: A

15. Project selection is done in which phase of the project work?

    A. Initiation
    B. Planning
    C. Execution
    D. Closure

    Answer: A

16. The project charter is developed in the:

    A. Initiation phase
    B. Planning phase
    C. Execution phase
    D. Closure phase

    Answer: A

17. A toy manufacturing company introduces a new model of toys, and you, as project manager, are assigned to outline the details of the launch. Your first task would be to:

   A. Start planning right away
   B. Conduct a requirements analysis
   C. Start execution when you feel the time is right
   D. None of the above

   Answer: B

18. When do you conduct a feasibility study?

   A. Initiation phase
   B. Planning phase
   C. Execution phase
   D. Closure phase

   Answer: A

19. When do you need to initiate a project?

   A. The project can be initiated immediately.
   B. Once the project goal and customer requirements are well known.
   C. Once the project is generally defined; project goals are not necessary.
   D. None of the above.

   Answer: B

20. In the initiation phase of the project, you:

   A. Develop the project management plan.
   B. Define the risks involved and perform contingency planning.
   C. Define the roles and responsibilities of the project stakeholders.
   D. None of the above

   Answer: C

21. In the initiation phase of the project, you determine the:

    A. Project objectives
    B. Resource performance
    C. Project risks
    D. None of the above

    Answer: A

22. The project charter is created during which phase of project work?

    A. Initiation
    B. Planning
    C. Execution
    D. Closure

    Answer: A

23. Creating a project title and description is a part of the:

    A. Risk management plan
    B. Cost management plan
    C. Project charter
    D. None of the above

    Answer: C

24. The responsibilities of the project manager are defined in the:

    A. Initiation phase
    B. Planning phase
    C. Execution phase
    D. Closure phase

    Answer: A

25. The project charter clearly defines the:

    A. Levels of authority within the project
    B. Levels of authority outside the project
    C. Levels of authority within the company
    D. None of the above

    Answer: A

26. A project charter:

    A. Requires approval
    B. Does not need approval
    C. May or may not need approval, depending on the project manager's point of view
    D. None of the above

    Answer: A

27. Which of the following deliverables describes your role as a project manager?

    A. Requirement document
    B. Project charter
    C. Cost analysis document
    D. None of the above

    Answer: B

28. Which of the following elements are part of the project charter?

    A. Project objectives
    B. Risk statement
    C. Quality statement
    D. None of the above

    Answer: A

29. In the initiation phase of project work, the following are not defined:

    A. Scope statement
    B. Feasibility activities
    C. Control activities
    D. None of the above

    Answer: C

30. When is the scope definition statement written?

    A. Initiation phase
    B. Planning phase
    C. Execution phase
    D. Closure phase

    Answer: A

PLANNING

PROJECT PLANNING

1. The project management plan is used to:

   A. Organize all the project activities per the triple constraint and in accordance with the project quality requirements
   B. Evaluate the performance of the team members
   C. Conduct project status meetings
   D. None of the above

   Answer: A

2. What does SOW mean?

   A. Section of work
   B. Statement of work
   C. Schedule of work
   D. None of the above

   Answer: B

3. Kick-off meetings involve:

   A. All stakeholders in a project
   B. The project manager and sponsor
   C. The project team
   D. None of the above

   Answer: A

4. Describe the planning phase of the project management process.

   A. The execution of the entire project is planned per the project requirements and in terms of the triple constraints.
   B. The project management plan is developed per the project requirements.
   C. Requirements gathering takes place.
   D. None of the above

   Answer: B

5. The project baseline is the:

   A. Original project plan with changes
   B. Original project plan without changes
   C. Original project plan yet to be developed
   D. None of the above

   Answer: B

6. Which of the following is not a feature of project planning?

   A. Time management planning
   B. Cost planning
   C. Quality planning
   D. Scope verification

   Answer: D

7. The project charter is approved and you are ready with the scope statement. What is the next step you will do as a project manager?

   A. Initiate the project
   B. Conduct planning
   C. Proceed to execution
   D. Close out the project

Answer: B

8. A kick-off meeting is the end of the:

A. Initiation phase
B. Planning phase
C. Execution phase
D. Closure phase

Answer: B

9. Why is a planning phase required in a project?

A. Planning is an essential component for any project. Without planning, the project is like a ship sailing in a sea with no destination.
B. Planning is a fundamental aspect of managing any project, small or large. Planning outlines what has to be done to accomplish certain goals.
C. Both A and B
D. None of the above

Answer: C

10. Which of the following statements is correct?

A. Project planning is an ongoing effort throughout the project work.
B. Project planning should take place before project work begins.
C. Project planning takes place in the execution phase.
D. None of the above

Answer: B

11. Developing the scope management plan is part of the:

A. Initiation phase
B. Planning phase
C. Execution phase
D. Project closure phase

Answer: B

12. Scope definition is done during which project phase?

A. Initiation
B. Planning
C. Execution
D. Closure

Answer: B

13. Creation of the scope management plan is done in the:

A. Initiation phase
B. Planning phase
C. Execution phase
D. Closure phase

Answer: B

14. Risk analysis is a part of:

A. Project initiation
B. Project planning
C. Monitoring and control
D. Closure

Answer: B

15. Resource allocation is a part of:

A. Project initiation
B. Project planning
C. Project execution
D. Closure

Answer: B

16. Identifying the project team and developing the project management plan is a part of which phase of the project work?

    A. Initiation
    B. Execution
    C. Planning
    D. Closure

    Answer: C

17. Contingency planning is a part of which project process?

    A. Initiation
    B. Planning
    C. Closure
    D. None of the above

    Answer: B

EXECUTION (MONITORING AND CONTROL)

1. During what phase of project management do you get a formal approval from the Change Control Board?

   A. Scope management process
   B. Risk management process
   C. Quality management process
   D. Change management process

   Answer: D

2. The CCB is the:

   A. Change Control Board
   B. Communication Control Board
   C. Cost Control Board
   D. None of the above

   Answer: A

3. Change requests are handled by:

   A. The Change Control Board
   B. Nonintegrated change control
   C. Quality control
   D. None of the above

   Answer: A

4. The term "change control" in a project refers to:

   A. Managing changes in the project
   B. Working as per the CCB guidelines
   C. Both A and B
   D. None of the above

   Answer: C

5. A project manager coordinates with the following entity to bring project changes under control:

    A. Change Control Board
    B. Project Making Committee
    C. Cost Monitoring Committee
    D. None of the above

    Answer: A

6. Approved change requests are specified in the:

    A. Monitoring and control phase
    B. Initiation phase
    C. Planning phase
    D. Closure phase

    Answer: A

7. In the monitoring and control phase:

    A. Quality analysis is performed.
    B. Corrective changes are made.
    C. Risk analysis is conducted.
    D. None of the above

    Answer: A

8. Change requests are implemented in the:

    A. Initiation phase
    B. Planning phase
    C. Monitoring and control phase
    D. Closure phase

    Answer: C

9. If the project work is going exactly as per the project plan:

   A. The project plan should be changed.
   B. The project plan need not be updated
   C. The project is well under control.
   D. Both B and C

   Answer: D

10. Managing risks and project issues is done in the:

    A. Initiation phase
    B. Planning phase
    C. Monitoring and control phase
    D. Closure phase

    Answer: C

11. Which of the following serves as a performance measurement tool?

    A. Project management plan
    B. Risk management plan
    C. Project status reports
    D. None of the above

    Answer: C

12. As a project manager on a time and materials project, you are having difficulty meeting project deadlines because of sudden system failure of an important software program. What should you do?

    A. You inform upper management immediately and try to find a solution to bring the project to a successful completion.
    B. You will be more concerned about your integrity in terms of delivery, so you will sign off immediately from the project without informing upper management.
    C. You try to locate a new software program with similar functionalities, no matter how much time it takes.
    D. You ignore the problem and carry on with other project work.

Answer: A

13. A periodic inspection is part of:

   A. Monitoring and control activity
   B. Risk mitigation activity
   C. Quality testing activity
   D. None of the above

   Answer: A

14. Performance measurement takes into account which of the following factors?

   A. Cost variances in a project
   B. Schedule variances in a project
   C. Both A and B
   D. None of the above

   Answer: C

15. Verification of project changes is a part of the:

   A. Project initiation phase
   B. Project planning phase
   C. Monitoring and control phase
   D. Project closure phase

   Answer: C

16. Monitoring project risk is included in the:

   A. Project initiation phase
   B. Project planning phase
   C. Monitoring and control phase
   D. Project closure phase

   Answer: C

17. Monitoring and control is:

    A. An important phase in the project management life cycle
    B. An optional phase in the project management life cycle
    C. An activity performed by a lower-level project team member
    D. None of the above

    Answer: A

18. Scope verification takes place during:

    A. Initiation
    B. Planning
    C. Monitoring and control
    D. Closure

    Answer: C

19. Change management:

    A. Involves overseeing and guiding the changes in project work.
    B. Refers to managing changes on the project team.
    C. Is the set of procedures developed to ensure that project design criteria are met.
    D. Is a mechanism to track budget and schedule variances.

    Answer: A

20. Cost control activity takes place in which phase of the project?

    A. Initiation
    B. Planning
    C. Monitoring and control
    D. Closure

    Answer: C

21. Controlling the changes that occur in project milestones or deadlines is called:

    A. Schedule control
    B. Cost control
    C. Quality control
    D. None of the above

    Answer: A

22. Who monitors and controls project changes?

    A. Project manager
    B. Customer
    C. Project team
    D. None of the above

    Answer: A

23. What is PMC?

    A. Project management and control
    B. Project monitoring and control
    C. Proper method of communication
    D. None of the above

    Answer: B

24. What is necessary to initiate the project monitoring and control process?

    A. Project management plan
    B. Risk management plan
    C. Quality management plan
    D. None of the above

    Answer: A

25. A project is monitored per the:

    A. Project management plan
    B. Risk management plan
    C. Communication management plan
    D. None of the above

    Answer: A

26. In the PMC process:

    A. Only the project manager is important.
    B. All project stakeholders are equally important.
    C. The project team is important.
    D. The customer alone is important.

    Answer: B

27. The project goal and deliverables are described in the:

    A. Scope document
    B. Project risk document
    C. Quality document
    D. Procurement planning document

    Answer: A

28. A project manager coordinates with which entity to bring project changes under control?

    A. Change Control Board
    B. Project Making Committee
    C. Cost Monitoring Committee
    D. None of the above

    Answer: A

29. Performance reports are:

    A. Risk evaluation tools
    B. Project monitoring and control tools
    C. Project data collection tools
    D. None of the above

    Answer: B

30. Project status meetings are conducted by the:

    A. Project manager
    B. Project team
    C. Customer
    D. None of the above

    Answer: A

31. Verification of project deliverables from time to time is part of the:

    A. Risk management process
    B. Quality management process
    C. Project monitoring and control process
    D. None of the above

    Answer: C

32. "Amount of rework" is a concern in the:

    A. Risk management process
    B. Project monitoring and control process
    C. Procurement management process
    D. None of the above

    Answer: B

33. Some of the inputs to project monitoring and control processes are:

   A. Cost estimates
   B. Schedule variances and critical path information
   C. Both A and B
   D. None of the above

   Answer: B

PROJECT CLOSURE

1. Project closure involves:

   A. Final sign-off on all project deliverables
   B. Final sign-off on just few deliverables
   C. The beginning of project closing activity
   D. None of the above

   Answer: A

2. Releasing project resources is a:

   A. Project initiation activity
   B. Project planning activity
   C. Project execution activity
   D. Project closing activity

   Answer: D

3. Formal approval on all project deliverables from the customer is a:

   A. Project initiation activity
   B. Project planning activity
   C. Project execution activity
   D. Project closure activity

   Answer: D

4. All of the following are closure activities except:

   A. Contract closure
   B. Formal sign-off
   C. Kick-off meeting
   D. None of the above

   Answer: C

5. Sue and Mike have subcontracted their wedding planning to a wedding service company, and all the service requests have been met as per the contractual agreement. This process is called:

   A. Administration of the contract
   B. Knowledge of the contract
   C. Contract closure
   D. None of the above

   Answer: A

6. Historical information is:

   A. Vital to project success
   B. A contributing factor in project failure
   C. Not of any value to the project work
   D. None of the above

   Answer: A

7. You are assigned as a project manager in a car manufacturing firm, and you refer to the past project records to assist with value analysis in the project work. What kind of records are you referring to?

   A. Historical records
   B. Project deliverables
   C. Status reports
   D. None of the above

   Answer: A

8. Administration closure is a part of the:

   A. Initiation phase
   B. Planning phase
   C. Execution phase
   D. Closure phase

   Answer: D

9. What happens in the closure phase of the project management process?

    A. Conduct formal closure of the project involving final sign-off on all project deliverables
    B. Fire the project resources
    C. Sign off from the work
    D. None of the above

    Answer: A

10. Closing the project through formal sign-offs on project deliverables from the client is a part of which process group?

    A. Initiation
    B. Planning
    C. Closure
    D. Execution

    Answer: C

11. It is good to rely on what kind of project data before beginning project work?

    A. Historical information
    B. Present data
    C. Friend's view
    D. None of the above

    Answer: A

12. The project manager must ensure that the project closure criteria are completely met:

    A. Before closing a project
    B. At the beginning of a project
    C. In the middle of a project
    D. None of the above

    Answer: A

13. Historical records are very useful for:

    A. Past projects
    B. Future projects
    C. Both A and B
    D. None of the above

    Answer: B

14. A large number of projects use the common information stored in a central repository or knowledge link in software firms. What is the term used for this situation?

    A. Knowledge management
    B. Knowledge taking
    C. Knowledge giving
    D. None of the above

    Answer: A

Knowledge Areas

SCOPE MANAGEMENT

1. The scope statement is an input in the:

   A. Scope definition
   B. Risk definition
   C. Quality definition
   D. None of the above

   Answer: A

2. Scope management planning is an input to:

   A. The project management plan
   B. Risk analysis
   C. Quality analysis
   D. None of the above

   Answer: A

3. The complete scope of the project is designed in the:

   A. Quality management plan
   B. Time management plan
   C. WBS
   D. None of the above

   Answer: C

4. How would you define the term "scope management"?

   A. Scope management ensures that the project addresses only the required work and no outside tasks.
   B. Scope management addresses all the work of the company, both internal and external to the project work.
   C. Both A and B
   D. None of the above

   Answer: A

5. The project goals and deliverables are described in the:

   A. Project risk document
   B. Quality document
   C. Scope document
   D. Procurement planning document

   Answer: C

TIME MANAGEMENT

1. Conducting status meetings is a must to know:

   A. The progress of the project
   B. Whether the project is a success
   C. Whether the project is a failure
   D. None of the above

   Answer: A

2. Proper planning in a project saves on:

   A. Cost management
   B. Time management
   C. Both A and B
   D. None of the above

   Answer: C

3. A WBS is created by the:

   A. Customer
   B. Sponsor
   C. Project team
   D. None of the above

   Answer: C

4. Activity definition is a method of:

   A. Identifying project activities
   B. Scheduling project activities
   C. Both A and B
   D. None of the above

   Answer: C

5. Activity sequencing is a method of:

    A. Arranging project activities sequentially
    B. Arranging project activities per their dependencies
    C. Both A and B
    D. None of the above

    Answer: C

6. Activity duration estimation is a method of:

    A. Estimating the time duration for each activity
    B. Estimating the total time duration for all project activities
    C. Estimating the initial time required for any one project activity
    D. None of the above

    Answer: A

7. Schedule development is a method of:

    A. Managing the schedule in a project
    B. Developing the schedule for activities outside the project
    C. Developing a risk plan
    D. None of the above

    Answer: A

8. The project schedule is an input to:

    A. Schedule development
    B. Activity duration estimation
    C. Activity scheduling
    D. None of the above

    Answer: A

9. The list of project activities serves as input for:

   A. Activity duration estimation
   B. Activity sequencing
   C. Schedule development
   D. None of the above

   Answer: B

10. What does ADM mean?

    A. Arrow drawing method
    B. Arrow diagrammatic method (of estimation)
    C. Activity duration method
    D. None of the above

    Answer: B

11. PDM stands for:

    A. Precedence diagramming method
    B. Project defining method
    C. Project duration method
    D. None of the above

    Answer: A

12. Activity on node is a:

    A. Precedence diagrammatic method
    B. Project risk estimation method
    C. Project quality estimation method
    D. None of the above

    Answer: A

13. The following are relationships in PDM:

    A. Finish to finish/finish to start
    B. Start to start/start to finish
    C. Both A and B
    D. None of the above

Answer: C

14. Delay in an activity from the start is known as:

    A. Slack time
    B. Lag time
    C. Both A and B
    D. None of the above

Answer: A

15. Activity resource requirements serve as input to:

    A. Activity sequencing
    B. Activity duration estimation
    C. Scheduling
    D. None of the above

Answer: B

16. Activity duration estimation is an input to:

    A. Project plan development
    B. Schedule development
    C. Cost estimation
    D. None of the above

Answer: B

17. The project schedule is an output of:

    A. The project management plan
    B. Schedule development
    C. Cost estimation
    D. None of the above

    Answer: B

18. CPM stands for:

    A. Cost project method
    B. Cost precedence method
    C. Critical path method
    D. None of the above

    Answer: C

19. Which of the following methods calculates the early and late start and finish for all project activities?

    A. Critical path method
    B. Non-critical path method
    C. Cost estimation method
    D. None of the above

    Answer: A

20. Gantt charts represent the activities present in the:

    A. WBS
    B. Risk plan
    C. Quality plan
    D. None of the above

    Answer: A

21. A Gantt chart shows project activities with:

    A. Horizontal bars
    B. Vertical bars
    C. Both A and B
    D. None of the above

    Answer: A

22. The following shows activities arranged sequentially in a network, representing the longest duration in a project:

    A. Critical path
    B. Gantt chart
    C. Status report
    D. None of the above

    Answer: A

23. Which type of graphic is a horizontal bar chart showing the project schedule?

    A. Gantt chart
    B. PERT chart
    C. Scatter diagram
    D. None of the above

    Answer: A

24. A task with zero duration is called:

    A. A project milestone
    B. A kill point
    C. Scope creep
    D. A quality metric

    Answer: A

25. Activity definition is a part of:

   A. Time management
   B. Cost management
   C. Quality management
   D. All of the above

   Answer: A

26. Ensuring that the project is completed on time is part of which project management process?

   A. Time management
   B. Cost management
   C. Quality management
   D. None of the above

   Answer: A

27. Activity definition is part of which project management process?

   A. Cost management
   B. Time management
   C. Quality management
   D. Risk management

   Answer: B

28. Schedule development is part of which project management process?

   A. Cost management
   B. Procurement management
   C. Quality management
   D. Time management

   Answer: D

29. Which activities are performed in the time management process?

   A. Activity definition and sequencing
   B. Activity duration estimation and schedule development
   C. Both A and B
   D. None of the above

   Answer: C

30. Schedule development is done:

   A. Before getting the final estimates
   B. After getting the final estimates
   C. While the final estimates are being submitted
   D. None of the above

   Answer: C

31. Gantt charts are used for:

   A. Schedule management
   B. Cost management
   C. Quality management
   D. Risk management

   Answer: A

32. Interdependencies between tasks are shown in a:

   A. Scatter diagram
   B. Project charter
   C. Gantt chart
   D. None of the above

   Answer: C

33. A Gantt chart is used to track:

    A. Project progress
    B. Project failure
    C. Project success
    D. None of the above

    Answer: A

34. "Slack time" is defined as:

    A. The time span in which the critical path can be delayed without affecting the project
    B. The time span in which the project is not delayed or affected by changes
    C. The time span in which changes affect the project timeline
    D. None of the above

    Answer: A

35. In the finish-to-start method of time management, a task finishes:

    A. Before the beginning of the next task
    B. After the next task begins
    C. At the same time as other tasks
    D. None of the above

    Answer: A

36. In the finish-to-finish method of time management:

    A. One task must finish before another.
    B. Both tasks finish at the same time.
    C. One task must finish after another.
    D. None of the above

    Answer: A

37. In the start-to-start method of time management:

    A. One task starts after the next task begins.
    B. One task starts before the next task begins.
    C. Both tasks begin at the same time.
    D. None of the above

    Answer: A

38. In the start-to-finish method of time management:

    A. A task should start before the next task finishes.
    B. A task should finish before the next task starts.
    C. A task should start at the same time as the next task.
    D. None of the above

    Answer: B

39. What does CPA mean?

    A. Critical path analysis
    B. Critical project analysis
    C. Critical project authorization
    D. None of the above

    Answer: A

40. Calculating the time allocated for completing each task in a project is performed during:

    A. Critical path analysis
    B. Risk analysis
    C. Quality analysis
    D. None of the above

    Answer: A

41. Which of the following updates the project manager about the project schedule?

    A. PERT chart
    B. Scatter diagrams
    C. Gantt chart
    D. All of the above

    Answer: C

42. A Gantt chart is used in:

    A. Project planning.
    B. Scheduling
    C. Risk planning
    D. Quality planning

    Answer: B

43. Which of the following is a status reporting tool?

    A. Gantt chart
    B. PERT diagram
    C. Scatter diagram
    D. None of the above

    Answer: A

44. Time management is:

    A. Managing time to accomplish a specific task in project work
    B. Conducting risk/value analysis
    C. Conducting quality analysis
    D. None of the above

    Answer: A

1. The WBS:

    A. Breaks down the project tasks to their simplest form
    B. Defines the number of project tasks
    C. Arranges the project tasks in order
    D. None of the above

    Answer: A

2. The WBS is created by the:

    A. Project team
    B. Customer
    C. Project manager
    D. None of the above

    Answer: A

3. The WBS does not include work:

    A. In the project
    B. Outside the project
    C. In the customer requirements
    D. None of the above

    Answer: B

4. The WBS provides the basis for:

    A. Project cost estimations
    B. Project time estimations
    C. Both A and B
    D. None of the above

    Answer: C

5. What does PERT stand for?

   A. Program Evaluation Review Technique
   B. Project Evaluation Result Technique
   C. Project Estimation Review Technique
   D. None of the above

   Answer: A

6. In what year was PERT developed?

   A. 1940
   B. 1950
   C. 2000
   D. 2006

   Answer: B

7. The basic aim of PERT activity is to:

   A. Reduce the time and cost of the project
   B. Reduce the resources of the project
   C. Reduce customer changes to the project
   D. None of the above

   Answer: A

8. Which of the following is an activity-based diagram?

   A. PERT chart
   B. Scatter chart
   C. Pie chart
   D. None of the above

   Answer: A

9. In a PERT diagram:

    A. Activity is represented by nodes, and milestones are represented by lines.
    B. Activity is represented by lines, and milestones are represented by nodes.
    C. Activity is represented by both lines and nodes.
    D. None of the above

    Answer: A

10. A PERT chart is also called:

    A. An activity-on-node diagram
    B. An activity-on-line diagram
    C. An activity line-node diagram
    D. None of the above

    Answer: B

11. In a PERT planning session:

    A. Activities are identified
    B. Activities are sequenced
    C. Both A and B
    D. None of the above

    Answer:C

12. Critical path analysis is the final activity in:

    A. A PERT chart
    B. A Gantt chart
    C. The project management plan
    D. None of the above

    Answer: A

13. In precedence diagrammatic method activities are represented on:
   A. Nodes
   B. Lines
   C. Nodes and lines
   D. None of the above

   Answer: A

14. Scope verification is:

   A. The process of final inspection and sign-off on project deliverables
   B. The same as initiation
   C. The same as management
   D. None of the above

   Answer: A

15. What does WBS stand for?

   A. Work breakout schedule
   B. Work breakdown structure
   C. Wide band structure
   D. None of the above

   Answer: B

16. Name the graphic tool used in breaking down project work into manageable units.

   A. WBS
   B. PERT chart
   C. Both A and B
   D. None of the above

   Answer: A

17. The WBS is created during which phase of project work?

    A. Execution
    B. Initiation
    C. Planning
    D. None of the above

    Answer: C

18. PERT is used for:

    A. Planning
    B. Measuring project performance
    C. Identifying project objectives
    D. None of the above

    Answer: C

19. Which one of the following activities addresses changes in the project scope?

    A. Measuring performance
    B. Making changes
    C. Taking corrective action
    D. Conducting requirements gathering

    Answer: C

COST MANAGEMENT

1. What does "cost variance" mean in project work?

    A. It is the difference between the budgeted and actual costs of the work.
    B. It is the actual cost of the work.
    C. It is the budgeted cost of the work to be performed.
    D. None of the above

    Answer: A

2. Parametric estimation is a part of:

    A. Cost estimation
    B. Risk estimation
    C. Quality estimation
    D. None of the above

    Answer: A

3. Cost baseline is an input for:

    A. Schedule development
    B. Quality estimations
    C. Cost budgeting
    D. None of the above

    Answer: C

4. "Estimates at completion" is an output of the:

    A. Time control process
    B. Cost control process
    C. Quality control process
    D. None of the above

    Answer: B

5. Which factor is used for measuring cost performance in project work?

A. Work breakdown structure
B. Project schedule
C. Cost baseline
D. Cost budget

Answer: C

6. Cost budgeting includes:

A. Cost estimates
B. Work breakdown structure
C. Both B and C
D. None of the above

Answer: C

7. The process of developing a cost management plan defines the method of:

A. Planning
B. Estimating
C. Controlling
D. All of the above

Answer: A

8. Parametrical estimation is a mathematical model used as a:

A. Cost estimation method
B. Quality estimation method
C. Risk estimation method
D. None of the above

Answer: A

9. Bottom-up estimation is performed during which process?

    A. Time management
    B. Cost management
    C. Quality management
    D. None of the above

Answer: B

QUALITY MANAGEMENT

1. Quality policies and procedures are included in the:

    A. Risk management plan
    B. Quality management plan
    C. Cost management plan
    D. None of the above

    Answer: B

2. Audits or regular checks are a method of:

    A. Quality control
    B. Quality assurance
    C. Quality planning
    D. None of the above

    Answer: A

3. Quality is considered to be achieved when:

    A. All the quality requirements of the project are met.
    B. The quality requirements of the project are partially met.
    C. The project work is completed per the quality standards and procedures of the organization.
    D. Both A and C

    Answer: D

4. Determining the quality standards and procedures and implementing them in the project are elements of:

    A. Quality assurance
    B. Quality control
    C. Risk analysis
    D. None of the above

    Answer: A

5. Which of the following takes place during the monitoring and control phase of a project?

   A. Quality audits
   B. Periodic inspections
   C. Project team building
   D. Both A and B

   Answer: D

6. In a project to develop a toy train for manufacture, the train must undergo testing to ensure its functionality. The testing phase is part of which project management process?

   A. Cost management
   B. Time management
   C. Quality management
   D. None of the above

   Answer: C

7. What is the outcome of quality planning?

   A. Quality management plan
   B. Risk management plan
   C. Procurement management plan
   D. None of the above

   Answer: A

8. Managing technical performance is most crucial for the:

   A. Sponsor
   B. Customer
   C. Project team members
   D. Project manager

   Answer: D

9. The quality management plan serves as input for:

    A. The quality control process
    B. Quality assurance
    C. Both A and B
    D. None of the above

    Answer: A

10. What is the role of the quality management process in a project?

    A. To ensure that the project is completed per the quality standards of the organization.
    B. To ensure that the project deliverables are completed per the project manager's standards.
    C. To ensure that the project is on schedule.
    D. None of the above

    Answer: C

11. The quality management process ensures:

    A. That the project work is not out of compliance
    B. That the project is completed within the timeline
    C. That the project is completed within the estimated cost
    D. None of the above

    Answer: A

12. What does the term "quality management" mean?

    A. Conformance to requirements
    B. Nonconformance to requirements
    C. Conformance to the project manager's standards of quality
    D. None of the above

    Answer: A

13. The output of quality planning is a:

    A. Risk plan
    B. Quality management plan
    C. Cost plan
    D. None of the above

    Answer: B

14. Quality management consists of the following processes:

    A. Quality planning and quality assurance
    B. Quality control
    C. Both A and B
    D. None of the above

    Answer: C

15. Quality management ensures that the project complies with the:

    A. Quality requirements of the organization
    B. Quality requirements of the project manager
    C. Quality requirements of the project team
    D. None of the above

    Answer: A

16. Quality control is done during which phase of project work?

    A. Initiation
    B. Planning
    C. Monitoring and control
    D. Closure

    Answer: C

17. Holding periodic inspections is part of:

    A. Quality control
    B. Change control
    C. Risk control
    D. None of the above

    Answer: A

18. To ensure the project is not out of compliance, verification of the quality standards takes place during which process?

    A. Risk management
    B. Cost management
    C. Quality management
    D. All of the above

    Answer: C

COMMUNICATION MANAGEMENT

1. Name the different types of communication.

    A. Direct/indirect
    B. Formal/informal
    C. Both A and B
    D. None of the above

    Answer: C

2. Communication gaps could be a result of:

    A. Improper communication among various project groups
    B. Lack of communication among various project groups
    C. Both A and B
    D. None of the above

    Answer: C

3. Conveying the "right" information to the "right" person at the "right" time is called:

    A. Cost management
    B. Communication management
    C. Risk management
    D. None of the above

    Answer: B

4. A project manager's role involves:

    A. 90% communication
    B. 10% communication
    C. 20% communication
    D. None of the above

    Answer: A

5. Which of the following is a formal method of communication?

   A. Technical presentations to project groups
   B. Project team get-togethers
   C. Project status meetings
   D. Both A and C

   Answer: D

6. The communication process involves:

   A. "What" needs to be communicated to "whom" and "how"
   B. What needs to be communicated
   C. Written communications
   D. None of the above

   Answer: A

7. Ensuring that information is communicated accurately to the right person at the right time is part of the:

   A. Communication management process
   B. Risk management process
   C. Cost management process
   D. Quality management process

   Answer: A

8. Communication requirements should serve as input to:

   A. Cost planning
   B. Time planning
   C. Communication planning
   D. None of the above

   Answer: C

9. One of the project manager's main responsibilities is to ensure effective:

   A. Communication among various project groups
   B. Risk planning
   C. Quality planning
   D. None of the above

   Answer: A

10. The phrase "right communication to the right person at the right time" describes which process area of project management?

   A. Risk management
   B. Quality management
   C. Procurement management
   D. Communications management

   Answer: D

HUMAN RESOURCES MANAGEMENT

1. The best approach to conflict resolution is:

    A. Direct communication
    B. Indirect communication
    C. Formal/informal/situational
    D. Both A and C

    Answer: A

2. A project manager must evaluate the project team in terms of:

    A. Performance
    B. Non-performance
    C. Both A and B
    D. None of the above

    Answer: C

3. In people management, a project manager needs to understand:

    A. His or her own personality and work ethic
    B. The personalities and work ethic of those on the project team
    C. Both A and B
    D. None of the above

    Answer: C

4. It is a good practice to be:

    A. A proactive project manager
    B. An active project manager
    C. A reactive project manager
    D. None of the above

    Answer: A

5. The staffing management plan is the output of:

   A. Risk planning
   B. Cost management planning
   C. Human resource planning
   D. None of the above

   Answer: C

6. Motivation is a method to:

   A. Ensure team development
   B. Develop a cost plan
   C. Develop a risk plan
   D. None of the above

   Answer: A

7. Performing is a part of:

   A. Team development
   B. Risk development
   C. Schedule development
   D. None of the above

   Answer: A

8. Which of the following is not the project manager's responsibility?

   A. Team building
   B. Resource allocation
   C. Communication not related to the project work
   D. Resolution of team members' personal problems

   Answer: D

9. Conflict management is a part of:

   A. Risk management
   B. Human resource management
   C. Time management
   D. Cost management

Answer: B

10. Team development involves:

   A. Identifying the project team
   B. Building the project team
   C. Both A and B
   D. None of the above

Answer: B

11. Building a positive attitude in the project team is the responsibility of the:

   A. Sponsor
   B. Customer
   C. Project manager
   D. None of the above

Answer: C

12. Conflict resolution is a part of:

   A. Cost management
   B. Risk management
   C. Quality management
   D. Human resource management

Answer: D

13. Which of the following is a part of project human resource management?

    A. Cost estimations
    B. Schedule estimations
    C. Resource estimations
    D. None of the above

    Answer: C

14. As a project manager, you:

    A. Motivate and build a strong project team
    B. Lead and encourage the project team
    C. Leave the team as it is
    D. Both A and B

    Answer: D

15. Which of the following contributes to team motivation?

    A. A rewards program
    B. Formal recognitions
    C. Both A and B
    D. None of the above

    Answer: C

16. As a good project manager, you must present yourself:

    A. With integrity and humility
    B. As inspiring and ethical
    C. As intimidating and unreceptive to suggestions or ideas
    D. Both A and B

    Answer: D

17. During a project discussion, you get the impression that a particular member of the project team is not performing well, although his past records show excellent performance. As a project manager, your first step would be to:

    A. Find the reason for the non-performance of the team member.
    B. Ignore the team member's non-performance
    C. Try to motivate the team member.
    D. Both A and C

    Answer: D

18. Inbound and outbound training is a part of:

    A. Human resource management
    B. Cost management
    C. Time management
    D. None of the above

    Answer: A

19. Maintaining individual integrity is a part of:

    A. Scope management
    B. Professional responsibility
    C. Societal maintenance
    D. None of the above

    Answer: B

20. A team member gives you misleading results about her assigned project task. Later, you find out the truth of the situation, although the project is not affected by the inaccurate report. What would you do as a project manager?

    A. Fire the team member immediately.
    B. Talk to the team member about her lack of honesty.
    C. Ignore the team member.
    D. None of the above

    Answer: B

21. As project manager, you should primarily be concerned about:

    A. Partial project delivery
    B. Making the project a success
    C. The project team's good health and prosperity, which will allow them to perform well in the project
    D. None of the above

    Answer: B

22. You are in the middle of managing a project when your friend, a senior manager, asks you to quit your current assignment and help him with his project. What do you do?

    A. You accept the offer happily because you will now be reporting to your friend.
    B. You find the offer unethical and refuse gracefully, explaining to your friend the complications involved in such an action.
    C. You simply ignore the offer and carry on with what you have been doing.
    D. None of the above

    Answer: B

23. As a project manager, you find that the funds allocated for resourcing in the project are more than what is required. What do you do?

    A. Inform senior management immediately
    B. Appoint more resources to balance the cost factor
    C. Keep the overage to yourself
    D. None of the above

    Answer: A

24. A team member is uncooperative in delivering on his assigned task. When you ask him about the problem, he gives vague excuses that are unrelated to the task. As project manager, what do you do?

   A. Fire him immediately.
   B. Try to reason out and resolve the issue immediately.
   C. Suspend the team member for some time to make him realize his mistake.
   D. Ignore him and try to do his task yourself.

   Answer: B

25. This process tells us how to "manage" the project team:

   A. Human resource planning
   B. Cost management planning
   C. Time management planning
   D. None of the above

   Answer: A

26. Team motivation is a responsibility of the:

   A. Project manager
   B. Customer
   C. Sponsor
   D. None of the above

   Answer: A

27. Having a group get-together is a:

   A. Non-social activity
   B. Team-building activity
   C. Pert activity
   D. None of the above

   Answer: B

28. Who is responsible for handling conflicts on a project?

    A. Project manager
    B. Team
    C. Customer
    D. None of the above

    Answer: A

29. Measuring performance and identifying the root causes of problems can both be seen as:

    A. Inappropriate action
    B. Continuous action
    C. Corrective action
    D. None of the above

    Answer: C

RISK MANAGEMENT

1. Which of the following is not a part of risk planning?

   A. Identification of risks
   B. Classification of risks
   C. Both A and B
   D. Contract closure

   Answer: D

2. Which document describes plans for handling uncertainties in a project?

   A. Risk management plan
   B. Quality management plan
   C. Procurement management plan
   D. None of the above

   Answer: A

3. Identifying potential threats to successful project completion is part of:

   A. Time management
   B. Risk management
   C. Cost management
   D. None of the above

   Answer: B

4. The first step in risk management planning is:

   A. Risk identification
   B. Risk monitoring
   C. Risk control
   D. None of the above

   Answer: A

5. Risk analysis is part of the:

    A. Cost management process
    B. Risk management process
    C. Quality management process
    D. None of the above

    Answer: B

6. A sudden increase in a cost factor:

    A. Is a threat to the project work
    B. Is not a threat to the project work
    C. Can usually be ignored
    D. None of the above

    Answer: A

7. As a project manager, what should you do if you discover a risk factor that will affect the project cost?

    A. Don't inform senior management, hoping that you'll be able to make up the cost in other project areas.
    B. Inform senior management and take immediate action to solve the problem.
    C. Inform the project team, but keep the information strictly among yourselves.
    D. None of the above

    Answer: B

8. Risk response development is a part of the:

    A. Cost management process
    B. Time management process
    C. Risk management process
    D. Procurement management process

    Answer: C

9. In which project phase is the risk management plan developed?

    A. Initiation
    B. Planning
    C. Execution
    D. Closure

    Answer: B

10. The risk management process involves:

    A. Risk identification
    B. Risk quantitative/qualitative analysis
    C. Risk response planning
    D. All of the above

    Answer: D

11. The risk management plan includes:

    A. Cost analysis
    B. Risk analysis
    C. Quality analysis
    D. None of the above

    Answer: B

12. Risk identification is included in the:

    A. Risk management plan
    B. Cost management plan
    C. Quality management plan
    D. None of the above

    Answer: A

13. Risk management is a process that tells you:

    A. How to manage risks in your professional life
    B. How the company will respond in a crisis
    C. How to manage risks in project work
    D. None of the above

    Answer: C

14. The risk management plan includes:

    A. Risk identification
    B. Risk response plan
    C. Risk control processes
    D. All of the above

    Answer: D

PROCUREMENT MANAGEMENT

1. In a fixed-bid contract:

   A. The buyer pays the total price to the seller.
   B. The buyer makes a partial payment, as negotiated with the seller.
   C. The buyer pays what he thinks the work is worth.
   D. None of the above

   Answer: A

2. In a cost-reimbursable contract, the buyer:

   A. Reimburses the seller for some of the costs incurred
   B. Reimburses the seller for actual costs
   C. Reimburses the seller for any costs
   D. None of the above

   Answer: B

3. The number of man hours is calculated in:

   A. A time-and-materials contract
   B. A fixed-bid contract
   C. Both A and B
   D. None of the above

   Answer: A

4. A fixed-bid contract is:

   A. Less risky than a cost-reimbursable contract
   B. Not a risky venture
   C. More risky than a cost-reimbursable contract
   D. None of the above

   Answer: C

5. A contract is an agreement on certain terms and conditions:

    A. Between the parties involved in the project work to ensure that the requirements for products or services are satisfied
    B. Between entities outside the project work
    C. Between the project team members
    D. None of the above

    Answer: A

6. The price of a residential home can be calculated as a certain amount per square foot of living space. Knowing this amount is part of:

    A. Requirements gathering
    B. Cost control
    C. Cost estimating
    D. Both A and B

    Answer: C

7. Which of the following is an input to the process of contract administration?

    A. The contract
    B. Any document or deliverable related to the project work
    C. Documents and deliverables outside of the project work
    D. None of the above

    Answer: A

8. A detailed description of products or services to be delivered per the supplier's contract is called a:

    A. Project management plan
    B. Statement of work
    C. Cost management plan
    D. None of the above

    Answer: B

9. Which of the following contracts involves less risk on the seller's side?

    A. Time and materials
    B. Cost reimbursable
    C. Fixed price
    D. None of the above

    Answer: C

10. The procurement management process relates to:

    A. Acquisitions, purchases, and vendor contract management processes
    B. Vendor contract processes only
    C. Purchases only
    D. None of the above

    Answer: A

Quick References

ID	Resource Name	JUL	AUG	SEP	OCT	NOV
001	Project Manager	110 Hrs	120hrs	160 hrs	160 hrs	154 hrs
002	Project Leader	90 hrs	96 hrs	98 hrs	98	98 hrs
003	Senior Developer	80 hr	90 hr	85 hrs	120 hrs	110 hrs
004	Developer	76 hrs	60 hrs	65 hrs	60 hrs	60 hrs
005	Test Lead	90 hrs	90 hrs	90 hrs	110 hrs	80 hrs
006	Test Analyst	40 hrs	55 hrs	40 hrs	60 hrs	40 hrs

QUICK REFERENCE–TABLE 1A: STAFFING MANAGEMENT PLAN

PROJECT INITIATION	PROJECT PLANNING	EXECUTION (Monitoring and Controlling)	CLOSURE
Starting a Project	Planning for execution	Executing as per planned while monitoring and controlling the project changes.	Formal closure (Project closing)

Table 2 A–PROJECT MANAGEMENT PHASES

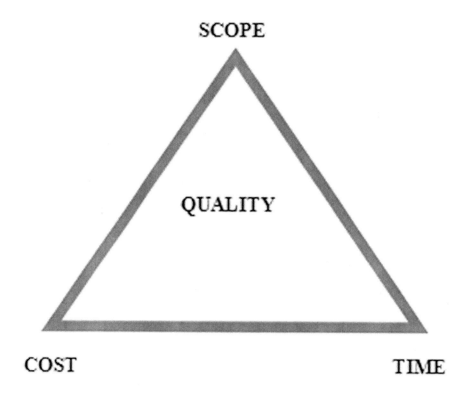

Figure 1 A : Triple Constraints

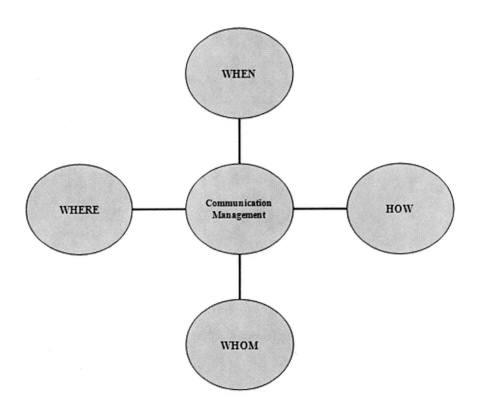

Figure 2 :A: Communication Management

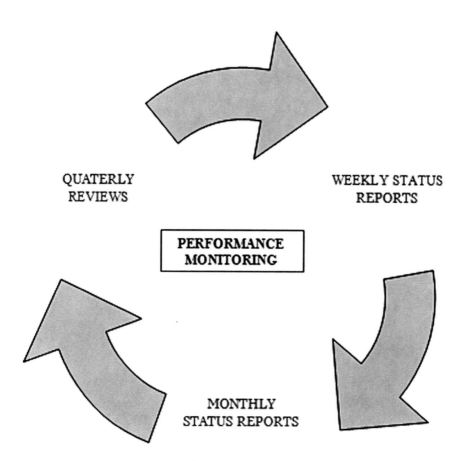

QUATERLY
REVIEWS

WEEKLY STATUS
REPORTS

PERFORMANCE
MONITORING

MONTHLY
STATUS REPORTS

Figure 3: PERFORMANCE MONITORING

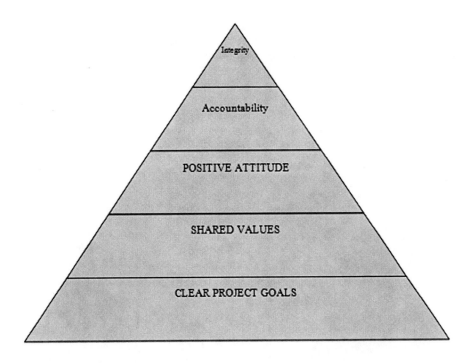

Figure 3A: Team Building

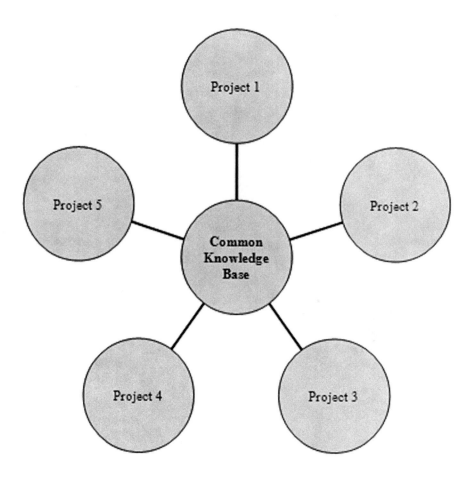

Figure 4: KNOWLEDGE MANAGEMENT

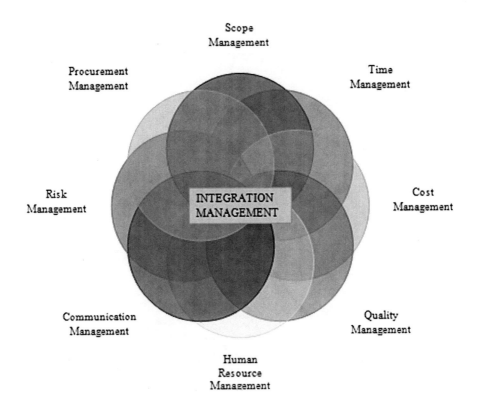

Figure 4 A–Project Management Process

Notes

Notes

Index

Page numbers in italics refer to tables and figures

Q

quality assurance 21,?22
Quality control 22
quality control 22

R

resource planning 19
risks 26,?38,?44
Risk identification 26
risk mitigation 25
Risk prioritization 26
Risk response planning 26
Role of the Project Manager 35

S

Scope 19
scope 19,?20,?38,?44
staffing management plan 22
statement of work 28

T

Team building 23
Time management 19
types of contracts 28

W

work breakdown structure
   19,?20,?21,?39

Breinigsville, PA USA
11 December 2009
229084BV00002B/13/P